P9-DEN-807

PROPERTY OF
ST. PAUL OF THE CROSS
LIBRARY

THE HIGH MIDDLE AGES

THE HIGH
MIDDLE AGES

A young people's pictorial history of the Church / volume three

Text adapted by Blanche Jennings Thompson from
THE CHURCH: A PICTORIAL HISTORY by Edward Rice

Farrar, Straus & Company / New York

by EDWARD RICE

PROPERTY OF
ST. PAUL OF THE CROSS
LIBRARY

1426

Copyright © 1954, 1955, 1956, 1957, 1958, 1959, 1960, 1961, 1962, 1963
by the A.M.D.G. Publishing Co., Inc.

Library of Congress catalog card number 63–9926

First Printing, 1963

Published simultaneously in Canada by Ambassador Books,
Ltd., Toronto

Manufactured in the United States of America

NIHIL OBSTAT:
   Edward J. Sutfin
   Censor Librorum

IMPRIMATUR:
 ✠ Robert F. Joyce
   Bishop of Burlington

The nihil obstat and imprimatur are official declarations that a book or pam-
phlet is free of doctrinal or moral error. No implication is contained therein
that those who have granted the nihil obstat and imprimatur agree with the
contents, opinions or statements expressed.

J
270
R

CONTENTS

THE FLOWERING OF

Of all the memorable phenomena of life in the Middle Ages, no two stand out more strongly than the Gothic cathedral and the crusades. The cathedral symbolizes the creative, imaginative drive toward the supernatural, while the crusades represent the active form of this striving—man's desire to gain a touch of sanctity by rescuing the sacred places of the Holy Land from the infidels.

By the twelfth century, barbarism had disappeared and the Europe of the new age was in a golden flowering never before experienced. Although man's physical condition was hardly better than before (housing was primitive; dirt, disease, superstition, and ignorance still left him prey to famine, plague, witchcraft, and other evils; and paganism was still widespread), in their own little corner of the world, a relatively small group of Christians produced a civilization whose art, literature, architecture, and creative thinking have never been surpassed. In addition to its intellectual and spiritual developments, the twelfth century was a time of many practical innovations throughout Europe. New cities sprang up, modern agriculture and commerce had their beginnings, and there was a great revival of monastic life.

THE MIDDLE AGES

*A forceful, new kind of sculpture, evoking a kind of
Christian joy, developed along with the Gothic cathedral.
These are figures from Chartres.*

THE GOTHIC CATHEDRAL

The Gothic cathedral, in France particularly, represented an entirely new approach to building. Whereas in the past most public buildings were massive walled enclosures, the Gothic builder made an open skeleton of stone which supported stone vaulting or arches. Each part of the building had a carefully calculated and important purpose, both structurally and artistically. The builders discovered principles of elasticity and balance which enabled them to achieve greater height and lightness. The pointed arch helped to decrease the lateral pressure caused by the immense weight of wall and roof and gave more flexibility in building. Extraordinary lightness of appearance was the result, and the builders grew constantly more daring, in spite of an occasional failure. (Part of the cathedral at Amiens, for example, collapsed because the vaulting was so delicate and the piers, or pillars, had to be doubled.) Other countries began building, and soon England, Germany, Spain, and Italy were imitating the inspired achievements of France.

A twelfth-century manuscript illumination (from the Guthlac roll) depicts monks building an English church.

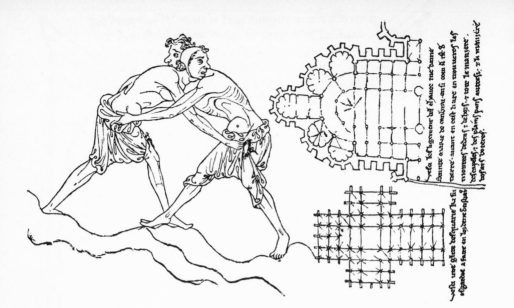

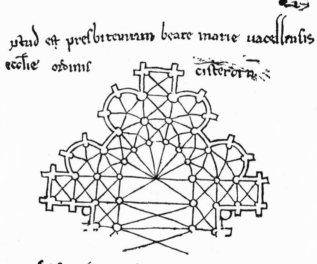

ptud est presbiterium beate marie uacellensis
ecclie ordine   cisterciu̅.

Ce est un imaudein si cume il est cheus.

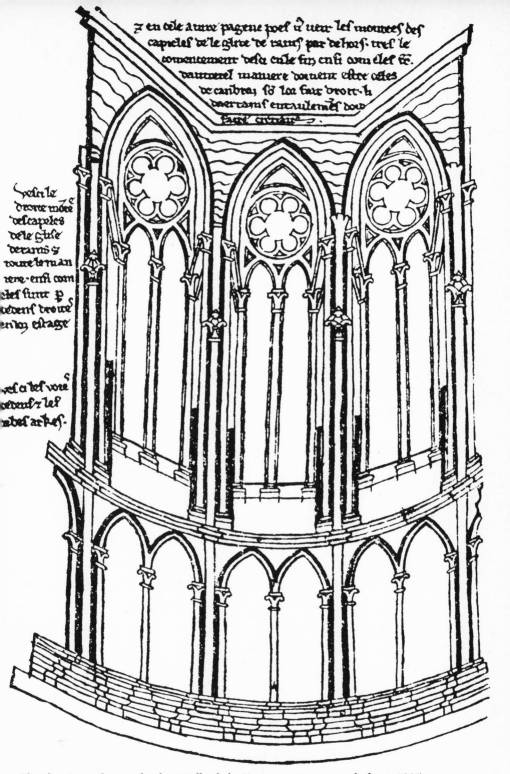

Sketches from the notebook of Villard de Honnecourt, prepared about 1235, describe in detail the construction of cathedrals. An architect, Villard was also skilled in geometry, masonry, carpentry and drawing. His notebook includes a disciple and a late Cistercian floor plan.

THE BUILDING OF CHARTRES

One of the most famous of all cathedrals is that of Chartres in central France. From the fourth century the town had been an episcopal see, and the original church had already been rebuilt several times as a result of fires. A final disaster in 1194 left nothing but a crumbling mass of stone. Dedication to the Blessed Virgin was widespread in France, and, as the people said, "Our lady must have a place of refuge." The cathedral, therefore, must be rebuilt. As far away as Normandy, people left their homes to go to Chartres and help with the building.

It was a strange and spontaneous migration. Roads were crowded with pilgrims, both men and women, dragging along huge tree trunks and great beams. Even the crippled and the sick were taken along. Their role was to pray while others worked. A city of tents sprang up around Chartres. The vast crowds of men, women, and children of all social conditions—knights, ladies, peasants, clerics, tradesmen—all submitted willingly to a self-imposed discipline, setting aside rank and calling.

The commune was self-organized. The workers elected their own leaders, who in turn were responsible to monk supervisors. (The name of the genius who designed the cathedral and supervised its construction is unknown.) The entire project was carried out in a spirit of sacrifice and penance. The greatest incentive of all was the honor of working on the new cathedral. So sacred was the enterprise that no one dared touch the material dedicated to the Blessed Virgin unless he had first confessed and reconciled himself with his enemies. Impenitent workers were expelled from the community.

The work progressed rapidly, and the cathedral, embodying the latest architectural and artistic concepts, was dedicated in 1260. It still remains one of the greatest glories of France.

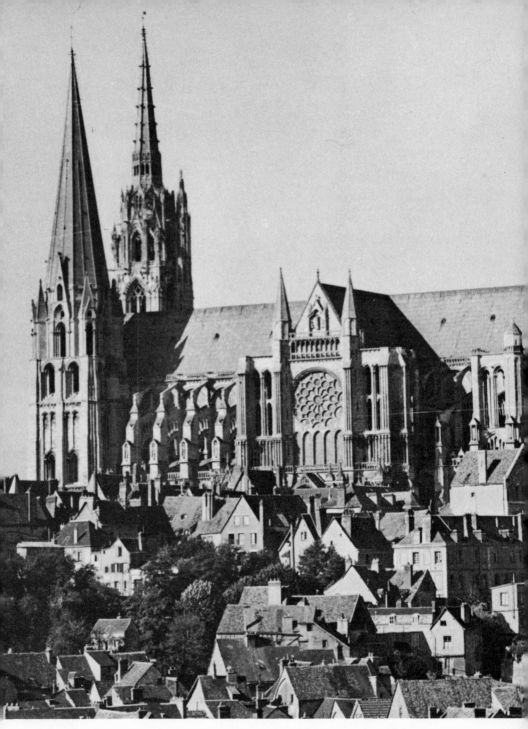

Symbolic of the flowering of medieval life in the twelfth century is Chartres
cathedral. Perhaps more than any other French cathedral, that of Chartres
approaches perfection. The upward sweep of her towers, her fine proportions, the
magnificence of her decorations evoke a spirit of Christian joy. The term "gothic"
was applied during the Renaissance to such architecture as a symbol of barbarism.

This is the central bay of the north or royal portal of Chartres. Dominating the composition is Christ enthroned, judging mankind. Around Him are symbols of the four evangelists. In the archings appear the elders of the Apocalypse, and below, the twelve apostles, grouped three by three. This portal was executed between 1140 and 1160 and is probably the greatest remaining example of Gothic sculpture.

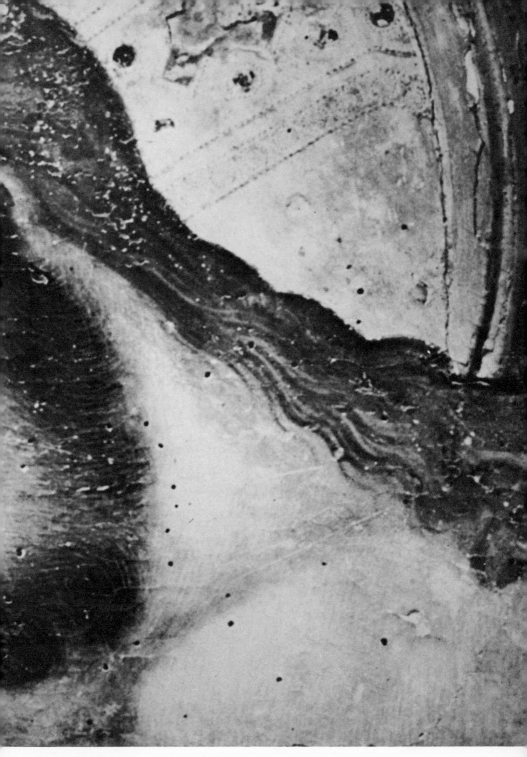

Cimabue, who is credited with this head of Christ (a detail of a fresco in the Sancta Croce in Florence), is put at the beginning of modern art. Born in 1240, he became interested in classical art and soon broke with the current Byzantine tradition then popular in Italy.

Duccio, a Sienese, climaxed the Byzantine tradition with a grave
and austere beauty and indicated a new direction for European
art. This scene is the calling of the apostles by Christ.

Giotto, a pupil of Cimabue, introduced naturalism into painting and gave passion and imagination to his scenes. The Ascension, one of a series of frescoes of the life of Our Lord, is in a chapel in Padua.

A NEW ECONOMY DEVELOPS

The West was basically an agricultural society when the Middle Ages began. Only in Asia Minor was there any important commercial activity. From such great seaports as Constantinople, cloth and foodstuffs were carried by Syrian ships to the West. But until the tenth century, the European city, as a center of commercial activity, did not exist. The town was merely a fortified stronghold. The key figure was usually the bishop, and the town population comprised chiefly people who were dependent on the Church for a living—clerics of the cathedral, monks, students, servants, and workers. Peasants came into town only on market days.

The horse collar, an important discovery, brought about a change in agriculture in the twelfth century; it enabled the horse to pull a bigger plow and also heavier wagons. Other innovations that aided economic progress were the rudder, developed in northern Europe, and from the East, the windmill, the paper-mill and the compass.

In the tenth century, however, a change began to take place. Merchants commenced to set up markets in the outer enclosures of the fortified towns, at bridgeheads or crossroads, or at the gates of monasteries and castles. Weavers, dyers, silversmiths, and other craftsmen moved into the market neighborhoods, and slowly a middle class began to emerge. The city just grew, unplanned and haphazard.

By the twelfth century there were great centers of commerce such as Venice, Milan, Florence, Siena, Marseilles, Barcelona, Ghent, Bruges, and Ypres. Certain towns in northern Germany formed a league for their own protection and soon established themselves as separate states. The city became a new way of life.

Serfdom was the lot of the common people of Europe. The serf was bound to work on land not his own—the manor—in a halfway state between freedom and slavery. Numerous customs and laws gave him a measure of protection, but his life was hard and short. The spread of a money economy broke down the manorial system and helped destroy serfdom. Life in the city began to develop. It was centered around a cathedral or a parish church. Outside the walls, merchants would set up stalls, which soon became permanent, and the old town would be swallowed by its FAUBOURGS. *European commerce benefited from the "Truce of God," a few days in each week during which Christians were forbidden under pain of excommunication to fight each other; a sudden boom in population also stimulated commercial activity.*

THE FIRST UNIVERSITIES

As Europe's horizons expanded, men began to have more leisure and more desire for knowledge and study. Although higher learning, in particular, was limited to a very few, there were still thousands of poor young men who were ready to endure any hardship in order to acquire an education. At its best, this was not easy. There were few texts. Many students, too poor to buy paper on which to write notes, were forced to rely on memory. Ordinary schools and even universities lacked benches, but the students were glad to stand or sit on the straw-covered floors. Schools began to arise everywhere, and at the Third Lateran Council in 1179, the Church ruled that every cathedral church should support a master who would instruct ecclesiastical scholars and give his services without charge to poor students. The medieval universities established a pattern of licensed masters, formal examinations, and the awarding of degrees. Some of the noted scholars of that period were St. Anselm, St. Bernard, Peter Lombard, St. Peter Damian, and the brilliant Peter Abelard who is regarded as the founder of the University of Paris, one of the outstanding schools of higher learning in the Middle Ages. Men like Abelard were practically one-man universities, so comprehensive was their scholarship, and young students made great sacrifices to study under them.

The University of Paris was one of the outstanding schools of higher learning in the Middle Ages. A manuscript illumination shows a special meeting of the faculty. The standing men hold scepters containing relics. Instruction was oral: the master read from the text and made comments from glosses written on the margins of the books. The word UNIVERSITAS *had nothing whatever to do with the supposed idea of universal knowledge. It was a common word in classical Latin for a guild or corporation; the University of Bologna, for example, was a guild of students; Paris, a guild of masters.*

THE CISTERCIAN REFORM

The great monastic system of Cluny had, in the tenth century, exerted tremendous influence for good, but as time went on it achieved too much power and too much wealth. The monks adopted the very things that their founders had rejected—soft furs on their robes, luxurious foods, and servants to do the unpleasant jobs. The monasteries were decorated with costly works of art, gilded statues, and mosaics. Worse than that, they had multiplied needless processions and unusual liturgical devotions so that true and simple worship had almost disappeared.

During the eleventh century a number of saintly men set out to reform monastic life. One of the most outstanding was St. Robert of Molesme, who was involved in the founding or reform of nearly a hundred monasteries. At Molesme he introduced the primitive Benedictine rule in all its powerful simplicity. Then he founded another house at Citeaux in a swamp in Burgundy. Eighteen months later, the Molesme monks begged for Robert to return; he did, and under him Molesme became an important Benedictine center. Citeaux might have disappeared entirely if it were not for St. Bernard, another of the reformers who exerted a great influence on the medieval Church.

Bernard was five years old when Pope Urban preached the First Crusade. His childhood ambition was to fight for the Holy Land. He was one of seven children, all of whom were well educated. Bernard's five brothers were trained as knights; because of ill health, Bernard could not serve as a warrior against the Moslems. Instead he was sent to a college for canons where young men were trained to serve on the staff of a cathedral or other large church. He was handsome, good-tempered, and popular, but after a brief show of worldliness, he grew more serious. At 22, he became interested in the monastery at Citeaux and persuaded four of his brothers and a number of other kins-

men, 31 in all, to enter the monastery with him. The group arrived at Eastertide in 1112.

All Bernard wanted to do was to disappear entirely and lead a life of prayer, but it was not to be so. Three years later he was sent out with twelve monks to found a new house in a lonely forest called the Valley of Wormwood. The monks were so poor that they sometimes lived on beech leaves and coarse barley bread. The harsh life caused Bernard's health to fail, but his monastery gained so great a reputation for holiness that it numbered 130 members and sent monks out to found other houses. So great was its fame that its name was changed to Clairvaux, meaning "illustrious valley." Bernard nearly died from too many vigils and too much fasting, but after a period of rest he was restored to health and became abbot of Clairvaux.

Under Bernard the Cistercians developed into a tremendous influence for good and an example of the monastic life at its finest and purest. By the end of the twelfth century they had 530 abbeys in France, the Netherlands, Germany, and England. They restored farming as a chief activity of monks and developed new agricultural techniques. They were also pledged to teach the ignorant and care for the poor. Each monastery had a house for the poor and an infirmary for the sick. Bernard became famous throughout Europe as a scholar, a preacher, and a miracle worker. He reproved the Knights Templar for worldliness and drafted a new rule for them. He helped Pope Eugenius preach the Second Crusade in 1145, traveling through France and Germany. Never strong, and often quite ill, he finally spent himself in his work and died in 1153 at the age of 63.

The swamps of Citeaux (from CISTELS, *or reeds) were reclaimed by Robert of Molesme and his monks. Throughout Europe, the Cistercians turned the wilderness into farmland and revolutionized agricultural techniques. Their* INSTITUTA *forbade the exploitation of serfs; neither were they allowed to live off parishes or other benefices. They supported themselves by their own labors, from their farms, herds and flocks, vineyards, orchards, forests, quarries and fishponds.*

Cîteaux today. When St. Bernard arrived here, the monastery bordered upon destitution. The Cistercians were influential for nearly two centuries, but then declined in numbers and fervor. A revival came in France in the seventeenth century with the reform at La Trappe, and recently again in America.

The Ruins of Mellifont, near Drogheda in Louth. Mellifont, the first Cistercian abbey in Ireland, was established by St. Malachy in the twelfth century. Its first abbot and monks were trained in France by Bernard of Clairvaux, a friend of Malachy's. The Cistercians helped stabilize monastic life in Ireland.

The valleys and mountains of northern Italy, near Turin,
became a refuge for the Waldensians after their banning
in the twelfth century. (This is one of their villages today.)
The Waldensians established themselves as a separate
religious body and attempted to proselytize among Catholics.
Throughout the Middle Ages, their efforts led to the
burnings and massacres of their members; in the sixteenth
century they established contact with the Reformation;
but continually at war with the Italian state, they did not
receive political and religious freedom until 1848.

FIGHTS WITH HERETICS

During the twelfth century, the Church was threatened by two powerful, heretical sects, the Albigensians and the Waldensians. Both sects were dangerous enemies of the Church. The Albigensians, who lived chiefly in southern France and northern Italy and were technically not even Christians, seized Church property by force and drove bishops and clergymen from their sees and churches. They believed in two gods, one good and one evil, one in control of the spirit and the other in control of the flesh, the two being in constant conflict with each other. They taught that Christ was just an ordinary man and that the whole visible world was evil.

The Waldensians, led by a well-to-do French merchant named Peter Waldo, initiated a so-called reform movement based on evangelical poverty. They were pacifists and led austere lives themselves. They denounced the local clergy and insisted that personal holiness and renunciation were more important than the reception of the sacraments. Many Christians were deceived by the false doctrine and believed that it stemmed from true Christian self-denial. The Waldensians denied the authority of the Church and taught that every just man could absolve, consecrate, and preach the Gospel without sacramental ordination. In 1184 they were condemned as heretics by Pope Lucius III, but they were never completely stamped out. (Waldensian villages still survive in northern Italy today.) In the early thirteenth century a "holy war" began against the Albigensians, who had absorbed many of the Waldensians into their ranks. It dragged on for twenty years, often marked by great cruelty and injustice and ended only when the Inquisition began.

CHURCH AND STATE IN CONFLICT

In 1188, Pope Clement III, realizing that strenuous action was necessary if the Church were to accomplish anything in the Holy Land, started the Third Crusade. He asked the three most powerful rulers of Europe to take the Cross. They were Frederick Barbarossa of Germany, Philip Augustus of France, and Henry II of England, who was later succeeded by his son, Richard the Lion-Hearted. Frederick entered enthusiastically into the endeavor, which was the most skillfully planned of all the crusades. He seized the initiative from the other two rulers and rolled up a string of victories while Saladin, Sultan of Egypt and leader of the Moslems, retreated, destroying every city and village behind him. But disaster now struck the Germans. Frederick, while bathing in an icy stream, suffered a stroke and died, a fortunate event for the Moslems. The French and English kings, who had spent the winter scheming against each other, joined forces to take the town of Acre in Palestine, after which Philip announced that he had fulfilled his vow and went home to France. Richard, a brave and hardy warrior, carried on for a time, but because of his personal friendship with Saladin he gave up a chance for a military victory and accepted a treaty promising free access by the Christians to the Holy Places. That was something, but not enough, and soon affairs in Palestine were as bad as ever.

Frederick Barbarossa (or Red Beard) the Holy Roman Emperor, attempted to restore Germany to the great position it held before Henry IV, but was in constant conflict with the papacy. Frederick is seen here in the guise of a reliquary for relics of St. John the Evangelist.

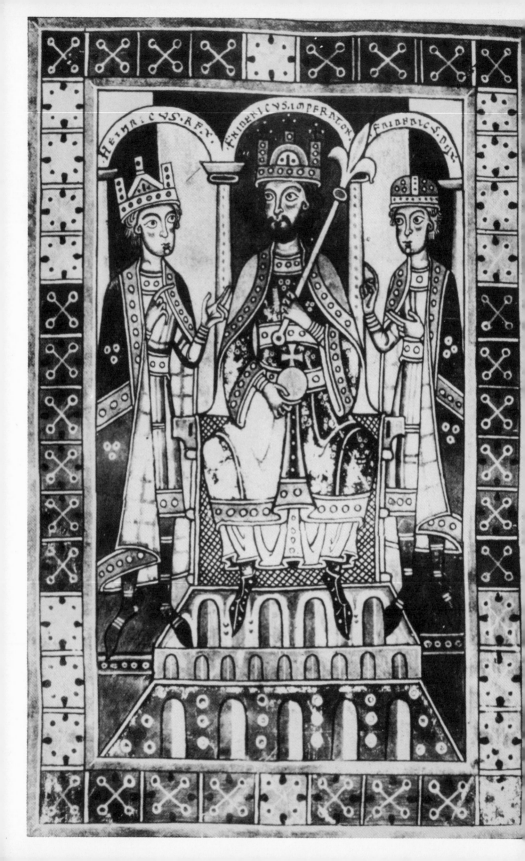

Frederick Barbarossa, shown here in a contemporary portrait with his two sons, Duke Frederick of Swabia and King Henry VI, was so typical a Germanic emperor that he seems more fictional than true. A handsome, impressive red-haired, well educated, courageous figure of great personal magnetism, he hated being thwarted and had a tremendous opinion of his powers and his rights.

His vassals pushed back both heathen Slavs and the Danes, colonizing their lands with Germans, and extending German power across the shore of the Baltic. The rest of his empire he either bought, married into, confiscated or took by force. His church policy was simple: to put into every empty bishopric one of his own candidates and to regard papal power as a threat to his own. Against the nobles his policy was similar: he tried to break up the great fiefs, creating a Germany of small principalities, bishoprics and free cities.

But in the English Pope, Adrian IV, Frederick met a will as hard as his own. The Pope needed Frederick's help against the Normans. Frederick wanted the Pope to anoint him Emperor. The Pope refused until Frederick, after bitter expostulations going on a day and a half, consented to hold his bridle and stirrup, thus bowing before the papacy. Though he experienced a humiliating defeat by the armies of Pope Alexander III, Frederick was a good enough Christian to be shocked by Saladin's victories in the Holy Land and to place himself under Pope Clement III for the Third Crusade. He scored some of his greatest victories against the Moslems with only 2,000 men.

Rīchardus rex angliæ . Ieruosolima rediens capt̄ p̄sentat augusto .

Rex angliæ d̄ morte oiachōis accusat̄ quod abnegās
se ensium manu excusaturū p̄mittit .

Tandē veniā petēns lit̄ absoluit̄

LEFT: *On his way home from the Third Crusade, Richard the Lion-Hearted was captured by troops of Leopold II of Austria. Leopold was forced to surrender his prisoner to the Emperor Henry VI (bottom panel), who in turn demanded a huge ransom from Richard, part of which was England itself. Richard's subjects raised the money and the king received his homeland as a fief (meaning that he ruled it, though the king possessed it).*
ABOVE: *The tombs of Richard and his queen, Eleanor. Richard was killed in a battle with Philip II of France. His death brought to a close the most vital era of European expansion into the Middle East, and, except for St. Louis later on, there were no major figures committed to the struggle against the Moslems.*

Typical of the new type of man to develop in the high Middle Ages was Frederick II. Though ruler of the Holy Roman Empire, he was by character and influence a Sicilian Norman; highly irreligious, he was accused of declaring that Christ, Moses and Mohammed were all impostors. He had the doubtful honor of having his excommunication the primary subject of discussion at the Council of Lyons. He is seen here with a favorite falcon.

the "greatest" of centuries

The thirteenth century was marked by rapid and profound changes in medieval society on many levels. The papacy, under Innocent III, reached the peak of its temporal glory. The feudal lord had attained the height of his power, having many of the privileges of sovereignty. He could hold court, mint money, set up markets, and levy tolls on roads and bridges. At the same time he was challenged by new concepts in government, particularly of the empire and the papacy. Possession of money was beginning to seem more important than that of land. New movements began in the Church under such leaders as St. Francis of Assisi and St. Dominic. St. Thomas Aquinas and other schoolmen were developing theological and philosophical studies. There was a new intellectual curiosity and an interest in the arts and sciences, resulting in part from contacts made with the Oriental world through the crusades and through the Arabs of Spain. The thirteenth century was an exciting time for men of all classes, and because of its concern with learning, with the arts, and with the human spirit, it stands as the greatest of medieval centuries.

difficilia emergunt circa negocia
huius artis. Regnauus aute[m] e[t]
numquam · nobilem h[ab]e[re] e[ss]e
er sola sua nobilitate uu[...] och
deuoli[...] et av augm[en]ti [...]im
pto i[p]m legi faciat[et] [e]xponi
mi[n]g bu[...] nobil[...]b[us] ad[n]a
cum ars [...] hu[...] n[o]bili[...]t[er] p
pria qu[a]d m[odo] tr[...] [et] c[etere] artu[m]
[et] nos non int[en]d[a]m[us] in o[mn]ia
d[e]i [...] l[ar]g[...] u[er]ba [co]uenient[...]
o[mn]ib[us] · [...] iu[n]ctio ill[...] [que] mag
indeuaricat[...] e[ss]e app[...]d p[...] qu[...]
[con]sell[...] g[...] poss[...]t iu[...] nr[i] · E[t]
h[...] [...] [...]o[...]
[.........hole.........]
[.........hole.........]
o[...] p[...] [...]
q[uo] p[...] u[...] p[...] p[...] R[ur]sus
[h]oia[m] pa[rs] d[i]g[er]etur i[n] d[i]scipli
[na] tam doctri[n]a q[uam] s[c]ien[t]ia ad
[...]o[...]a[...] s[ecundu]m q[uod] s[c]ien[tia]
ar[...] p[er]tin[...] · s[ecundu]m c[...] de
sp[e]cial[...] [con]s[i]d[er]at[...] h[...] [con]si[de]r[...]
Int[en]cio u[er]o i[st]a e[st] ma[n]ifesta[r]e
in hoc lib[r]o de uenat[i]o[n]e aui[um]
ea que sunt sicut sunt · [et] ad ar
tis cen[...]io[n]em rediger[e] quo[d]i[...]
null[...] h[abuit] s[c]i[enti]am hacten[us] n[...]
[...]ntem · Modus agendi [est] pl[a]
ctus prol[i]xitat[...]s · [et] e[xe]cutiu[us] e[x]
cut[i]u[us] u[er]o multipl[ex] partim
nam[...] diuisiu[us] partim d[e]scrip
tiuus partim [con]uenienti[a]m e[...]

dic[...] e[...]g[...] d[...]s · [et] c[er]ta[m] caus[a]m
i[n]quiri[...] · Et [...] hui[us]modi [h]is
s[e]q[ui]m[ur] [...]c[...] in u[i]u[o] p[...] [...]ro[...]
ur i[n]q[ui]sit[i]or · p[...] qu[...] ip[s]e am[at]or
diuine augusta[...] fr[e]d[er]ic[us] s[e]cun
dus roma[n]o[rum] imp[er]ator ier[usa]l[e]m
[et] sicilie [re]x · Utilitas e[st] magna · [et]
enim nobiles [et] pot[en]tes s[e] soll[...] cir
ca regimina mu[n]dano[rum] per huius
artis usum suis curis plen[i]usq[ue] i[n]
gaudiis nob[...] exerceo · Pauperes u[er]o
[et] mi[nus] nobiles d[...] hac arte nobili
bus seruientes obtineb[un]t ab ip[s]is
necessaria sue uit[e] · Utrius[que] u[er]o
b[e]ne arg[ume]n[tum] h[ab]et · Man[i]festa[...]
[co]ntent[i] op[er]at[i]o[n]is [...] in d[...]
u[...]r · Suppos[ui]m[us] [...] [sci]en[ti]
a[c] nat[...] la[...]e c[...] [...]da[...]
manifest[...] · L[...] re alie n[atur]e ex p
ci[m]ento p[er] bo[n]u[m] suu[m] hab[i]t[u]
altera[m] q[...]da[m] [m]odo u[ide]l[icet] nat[um]
[et] latu[...] culus[...] e[st] · Lib[er] du[...]
augusti f[r]id[er]ici s[ecundus] noma
lio[ru]m [...]g[a]r[...] ier[...] [et] sicilie
[re]gis d[e] art[...] [...]u[...]di cum aui[bus]
diuisiu[us] [est] p[...] a[...]o ad ma
nifestat[i]o[n]em ou[...] [...] natu
ra[m] uenat[i]o[n]e q[ue] sit p[er] aues ·
V[er]o ac[...] o n[...] sing[u]lis p[ar]tic[u]l[is]
euiden[...] p[ar]t[...] · P[r]ol[o]g[...]um
na[...] a[...] n[...]d[...] na[...]ab[...]u[...] · In
[...] u[er]o seu i[n] [...]at[i]o[n]e
e[...] [...]a[...]a sicu[t] p[ro]nu[n]cia
[...]r[...]s e[st] [que] s[ecundu]m na[...]
ra[m] [...] sicut p[ro]nu[n]t[ur] h[iis] q[ui]

THE HARSHNESS OF LIFE

Life for thirteenth-century peasants was as hard as it had ever been in the past, but an increasing number of them were beginning to free themselves from the land and establish themselves in the cities. A middle class of tradesmen, skilled craftsmen, and merchants was growing up. With the feudal lords so frequently away on crusades, the towns began to prosper. Craft guilds came into existence, replacing the merchant guilds. The new guilds set high standards of work and fixed ceiling prices, forbade unjust practices such as cornering the market, and provided a simple kind of social insurance in the form of death benefits for widows and orphans. New materials flooded Europe. To the wool trade, which had been developed by the Cistercians in the previous century, were added cotton, muslin, and damask. Better techniques of navigation and the development of new instruments resulted in larger ships and more daring voyages, as well as greater cargoes.

At first, not many benefits filtered down to the peasant. He lived a simple life, hardly better than the animals he cared for, ate crude food, and was freed from the monotony of his existence only by the frequency of the feast days that filled the Church calendar. The poor had little food other than peas, beans, cereal, porridge,

The work day for the land-bound was long and arduous. The Italian peasants shown here are beating rye with fla'ls. Rye, the medieval world believed, was "good for reducing humors, but it occasions color and melancholia. This can be remedied by mixing wheat with it."

Silligo

and weak beer to drink, and occasionally a little meat such as rabbit or fowl.

The rich set a better table. Beef, mutton, and pork, chickens, geese, and wild game were their regular fare. Meat was boiled or roasted and served directly from the fire on skewers. Chunks were cut off and eaten with the fingers. In the autumn, animals were killed and the meat salted down. Little was known about preservation, and strong spices were used to disguise the taste of decayed meat. For all classes vegetables were available, but many that are considered edible today were then classed as herbs and roots that only the starving would eat.

Among the upper classes food was served in appetizing ways and, considering the times, with a good deal of imagination. One monastic dinner given to entertain St. Louis and his followers (among whom were a cardinal, an archbishop, and other ecclesiastical and civil dignitaries) included: ". . . cherries; the most excellent white bread; choice wine, worthy of the king's royal state . . . fresh beans boiled in milk, fishes and crabs, pastries, rice cooked with milk of almonds and cinnamon powder, eels baked with a most excellent sauce, tarts, cheese, and all the fruits of the season in abundance and comely array."

Illustrations from a medieval manuscript show typical scenes of peasant life. TOP: *a young man bets on a borrowed garment and loses it to a gambler.* MIDDLE: *the principle of credit: payment passes from one group to another through a middleman. The bottom panel depicts a common right of the road: a traveler may cut as much grain for his horse as he can reach standing in one place.*

PROPERTY OF
ST. PAUL OF THE CROSS
LIBRARY
1426

*Innocent III as he looked
during his lifetime.*

A POPE FIGHTS THE KINGS

In the history of the papacy, Innocent III stands as a gigantic figure. He was elected in 1198 at the age of 37, and from the beginning believed that the pope was not only the ecclesiastical but the political head of the Church. One of his first acts was to acknowledge Frederick II, the grandson of Frederick Barbarossa, as King of Sicily. Frederick became the pope's ward and was educated for the imperial throne. In 1211 Innocent excommunicated the emperor Otto IV and saw to it that Frederick was elected in his place. When King John of England, the brother of Richard the Lion-Hearted, after years of rebellion and bitter resistance to the pope's spiritual power, challenged his nomination of Cardinal Langton as Archbishop of Canterbury, the pope put England under interdict (a severe ban by which the people are deprived of many of the sacraments, of participation in religious services, and of Christian burial), excommunicated John, and formally deposed him. The barons and the people supported the pope, and John was obliged to submit. He declared himself a vassal of the pope in return for the territory of England and Ireland, and agreed to pay a large annual tribute to the Holy See. Pope Innocent initiated the Fourth Crusade and later the European Crusade against the Albigensians. He gave the first approbation to St. Dominic's missions and to the preaching order of St. Francis of Assisi, and his greatest triumph was the Fourth Lateran Council, the most important synod of the Middle Ages.

Two important Church councils were held in the thirteenth century: the Fourth Lateran Council, held in 1215, commonly known as the "Great Council," brought together some 1,400 leading ecclesiastics to discuss pressing problems. Seventy canons on Church government and discipline were ratified, and important doctrinal subjects were discussed (the term "transubstantiation" was used here for the first time), as well as relations between the Greek and Latin churches; the doctrines of the Albigensians, Waldensians and other heretics were condemned; the secrecy of confession was formally initiated. The Council of Lyons [LEFT] was called in 1245 by Innocent IV to deal with what he called "the five wounds of the Church"—the bad lives of the clergy and the faithful, the danger of the Saracens, the Greek schism, the invasion of Hungary by the Mongols and the quarrel with Frederick II.

A NEW CRUSADE

Innocent III was faced with the task of persuading a reluctant Christendom to enter upon a crusade that would put an end, once and for all, to the Moslem occupation of the Holy Land. He finally whipped together an acceptable crusading army, but the crusaders this time acted very little like men on a holy mission. In return for ships from the Venetians, they destroyed the city of Zara on the Adriatic, Venice's rival city. Then they went on to Constantinople. Overcome by the riches of that glorious city, they took it by force and set up a puppet government.

The citizens of Constantinople rioted against their captors in July, 1203, thus giving the crusaders a pretext for a three-day sack of the city during which even the churches were desecrated. Loot from the city's treasures and from the empire decorated all of Europe. The famed bronze horses that stand before St. Mark's in Venice, for example, were taken from the Hippodrome in Constantinople. The pope wrote angrily: "These soldiers of Christ who should have turned their swords against the infidel have steeped them in Christian blood." The crusaders stripped the altars of silver, violated the sanctuaries, and carried off crosses, ikons, and relics. Instead of marching to free the Holy Land, the crusaders now drove out the Greek nobles and clergy and set up a Latin Kingdom of Byzantium, which was badly managed and corrupt. The Fourth Crusade was a dismal failure, but Pope Innocent continued his efforts to unite Christendom against the Moslems to the very day of his death.

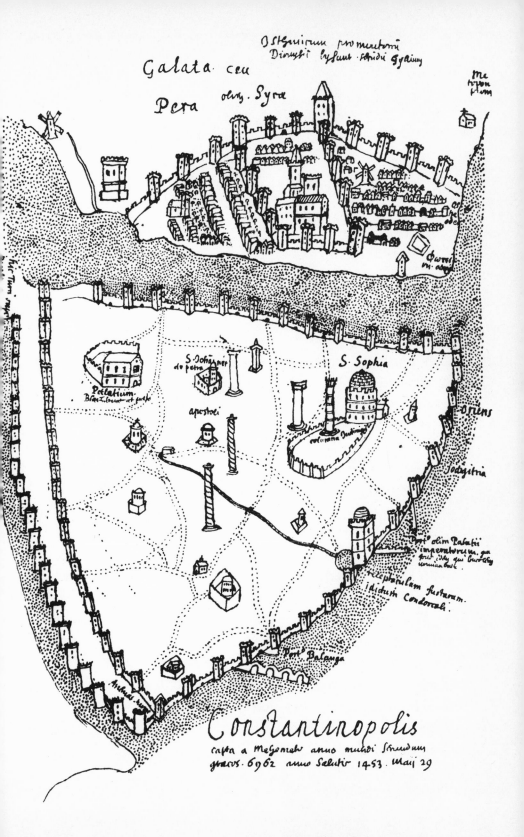

Galata ceu

Pera olim. Syra

Ostgenirum promentorii
Dionysti lyssant scridii Gyllinii

me
tropon
lium

S. Johanner
do petra

S. Sophia

Pallatium
Blac. Iheni at perh.

apostoi

columna Iustiniani

Oriens

Iodigitria

olim Palatii
imperatorum. qui
pars idg qui turolog
termine ouit

Cephonidam Rustaron
ichduni Condocrali

Port Balanga

Michael port

Constantinopolis

capta a Mehomete anno mundi secundum
graeos. 6962 anno Salutis 1453 Maij 29

For nine hundred years the St. Mark's horses stood in the
Hippodrome in Constantinople before being stolen by a
Crusader named Enrico Dandolo, doge of Venice, who placed
them over the central door of his city's basilica.
Originally they were cast in Corinth, Greece, about 200 B.C.
and most likely formed a group with a chariot. Nero
brought them to Rome in 68 A.D. to adorn
his triumphal arch on Capitoline Hill. In looting the Empire
in 330 for suitable ornamentation for New Rome, Constantine
took the group to his capital. In 1797 Napoleon stole
them to place atop the Arc du Carrousel in Paris. After his
exile, they were returned to Venice.

THE SAINTLY KING LOUIS

In the year 1212, almost fifty thousand children, nearly all French and German, set out for Palestine led by two shepherd boys named Stephen and Nicholas. Nicholas said that an angel had ordered him to free the Holy Places. The children marched across the Alps to Genoa, singing hymns. The people watched them go, hoping that youth and innocence might accomplish what greedy men and military strategy had failed to do. Of course, the crusade of the children ended in tragic failure. Many of them died of cold and hunger on the way, and others were sold as slaves to the Saracens. A sixth crusade brought only temporary success.

Finally there appeared the one man who brought to the scene all of the old fervor, sanctity, and spirit of the First Crusade. He was Louis IX of France, one of the Church's greatest saints. He had the enthusiasm of the true crusader. Before he departed he made a pilgrimage to the abbeys of his country, barefoot and carrying the traditional staff and scrip, to ask prayers for the success of the crusade. After a weary voyage across the Mediterranean, St. Louis and his fleet easily captured the city of Damietta, east of Cairo, but he failed to follow up his victory. The crusaders were unable to penetrate the maze of canals and swamps around Damietta. The army was demoralized by typhus and scurvy. Louis fell sick, his men were routed and slaughtered by the Turks, and he was captured while lying in a fever on a pallet in a mud hut. After being ransomed at an exorbitant price, he went to the Latin Kingdom of Byzantium and was installed as its ruler. (There were two medieval orders for the ransom of captives, the Trinitarians and the Order of Our Lady of Mercy.) Although he stayed there for four years, he refused to beg permission of the Moslems to visit Jerusalem, so he never did see the Holy Places. Finally, as unsuccessful as the children had been, he returned to France to plan a new crusade.

Louis IX "had the face of an angel, and mien full of grace," wrote Salimbene. "The King was spare and slender, somewhat lean and of a proper height. He came [on foot] to our church, not in regal pomp, but in a pilgrim's habit, with the staff and the scrip of his pilgrimage hanging at his neck, which was an excellent adornment for the shoulders of a king . . . his blood brethren, who were three counts . . . followed him in the same humble guise. In truth, he might rather be called a monk in devotion of heart, than a knight in weapons of war."

PROPERTY OF
ST. PAUL OF THE CROSS
LIBRARY 1426

St. Louis lands at Damietta in an attempt at breaking Moslem power. The landing was successful, but the crusaders lacked the will to capitalize upon their victory.

A somewhat fanciful map of the Mediterranean, prepared for the cause of St. Louis, shows his campaigns against the Moslems. In the bottom left he is seen dying at Tunis.

THE EVIL EMPEROR FREDERICK

No two medieval rulers were less alike than Frederick II, the Holy Roman Emperor, and Louis IX, King of France. Frederick had a brilliant mind, but he was completely irreligious. He had no faith in God and was interested only in worldly affairs. Louis was a simple man, kindly, courageous, and devoted to the Church and the papacy. A Franciscan friar described Frederick as crafty, malicious, and ill-tempered, yet kind and courteous when it suited him to be so. He was gay, sociable, and clever and knew how to read, sing, and play a stringed instrument. He could speak several languages and, the Franciscan adds, "If he had been rightly Catholic and had loved God and His Church, he would have had few emperors his equal in the world."

It was expected of every medieval ruler that he embark upon a crusade to fight for the Holy Land, but Frederick saw no gain for himself in such a luckless adventure, and he was excommunicated on three different occasions for his behavior in the crusades. From his earliest years he was engaged in struggles against kinsmen, against the Church, against other nobles, and against the free city states of Italy. His talents should have led to real greatness: he was keenly interested in science, medicine, astronomy, and astrology, and even wrote a treatise on hawking that was the first study of the anatomy and life of birds in modern ornithology.

In the secular world Frederick's most important work was the creation of the first modern state. There was nothing feudal in his administration of Sicily, which was his favorite domain. He developed the idea of a strong state supported by taxes and efficiently run. He encouraged commerce. Agriculture and industry flourished under his rule. He was a natural dictator who believed in strong governmental control of trade, restriction of civil liberties, and terrorization by a ruthlessly inhuman police force. Frederick was a remarkable ruler, but he never achieved greatness.

A falcon, the king of birds, from
the court of Frederick II,
ruler of the Holy Roman Empire,
is symbolic of his position
in medieval society. Like the falcon
which despises all other birds,
Frederick looked down on
the common lot of men;
he used the bird
as his symbol everywhere.

THE CRUSADES END IN FAILURE

Now another figure appeared on the scene to confuse the drama that already entangled Frank, Greek, and Moslem—the Mongol. A small warlike tribe that sprang unknown out of central Asia, the Mongols (incorrectly called Tartars by Europeans) swept without warning across China to the Pacific under the great Genghis Khan and suddenly found themselves rulers of half the world. While the crusaders were looting Byzantium, the Mongols were moving westward, murdering men, women, children, and even animals, in a terrific wave of destruction. Large parts of the Moslem world fell to the Mongols who, riding their strong, stocky little horses, hunted down Chinese, Persians, Russians, and Hungarians as other men hunted wild game. Reaching the Volga River, the Mongols were delayed briefly by the death of Genghis Khan, but his two sons soon resumed the campaign and headed for Vienna.

Curiously enough, many of the Mongols were nominal Christians who had been converted long before by Nestorian missionaries. Though heretics, they were properly baptized, and they often spared Christians while Moslems were ruthlessly annihilated. There were factions among both Mongol and Western warlords who thought it possible to unite in a common effort against the Moslems. Some progress was made in that direction, but the Latin barons at Tyre refused the alliance. They preferred to deal with a new dynasty in Egypt, called the Mamelukes, but the Mamelukes turned against both Christians and Mongols and drove the Mongols back into Persia.

Then came the Eighth—and last—Crusade. It was led again by St. Louis, who unwisely headed for North Africa instead of the Holy Land and landed in Tunis, hoping to convert the ruler there. The frightful heat sapped the strength of the crusaders. An epidemic broke out, and Louis fell ill, dying on August 25, 1270.

*Masters of half the world, the Mongols swept down on Asia
Minor and Europe, shooting Russians, Turks and Hungarians from
horseback like animals. Their threat to
the West ended when all their forces went home to select a
new khan. They never returned.*

The situation in the East grew steadily worse. The Mongols wanted the Christian leaders of Europe to join them in an attack against the Moslems, but only a few Armenians and Syrians responded. The attempt was a complete failure. The Mamelukes destroyed every remaining Christian outpost, ending with a terrible massacre at Tyre in 1291, in which 20,000 Christian defenders were overwhelmed by 100,000 Moslems. The crusades were over.

CHANGES IN THE LITURGY

The thirteenth century was a time of great devotion to the Holy Eucharist. The Sacred Host was by then being held up after the Consecration for the people to see and adore, but the practice of receiving Communion was rare. Even St. Louis, who attended at least one Mass every day, communicated only six times a year. The Lateran Council of 1215 sanctioned the minimum of a single annual Communion at Eastertide.

During the reign of Innocent III, a number of minor changes were made in the Mass as well as in the Divine Office. Two or three additions were made to the Mass, notably the *Judica me* psalm and the *Confiteor* at the beginning. By this time the Divine Office included the feasts of over 150 saints, and the list of required prayers was constantly growing. Pope Innocent edited the Office and published it as a single book called the Breviary. In 1241 the Franciscans revised it, and eventually the private recitation of the canonical hours—the divisions of the Breviary were so called because each one was to be said at an assigned hour—was required of monks when they were unable to recite the Office in choir with the rest of the monks. A number of liturgical hymns also date from the thirteenth century. Some of those still in use are the *Pange Lingua and Adoro Te* of St. Thomas Aquinas, the *Stabat Mater* and *Dies Irae*, written by Franciscan friars, and the *Jesu Dulcis Memoria, Alma Redemptoris Mater,* and *Salve Regina.*

The rite of ordination received special attention in the thirteenth century. Saints Bonaventure, Albert the Great, Aquinas and Duns Scotus all wrote about the sacrament at length. Here a bishop and ordinand are shown during the rite as practiced in the Middle Ages.

THE DOMINICANS COME INTO BEING

Much of the religious fervor of the thirteenth century resulted from the rise of the mendicant, or begging, orders known as Dominicans and Franciscans. St. Dominic, who founded the Dominican Order, was a Spaniard of noble birth named Domingo de Guzman, whom Pope Innocent III sent to France to preach to the Albigensians. With a rule of absolute poverty, Dominic and his companions wandered about Languedoc, preaching wherever they could. They were the first Catholic missionaries to achieve any success with the Albigensians.

In 1216 Dominic was given a house and church for his followers. Pope Honorius III approved his plans for a new order, which had the vocation of studying and preaching. Working closely with the newly founded Friars Minor, or Franciscans, the Order of Preachers spread all over Europe, attracting to its ranks some of the most brilliant intellects in Europe and founding houses in almost every Christian country. In 1233 Pope Gregory IX commissioned the Dominicans to investigate the secret practices of the Albigensians, who remained active in spite of persecution. This was the beginning of the Inquisition or Inquiry which became one of the most controversial actions ever entered upon by the Church.

A Second Order for women, which was eventually started, took over the education of girls, and a Third Order comprised men and women living in the world but desirous of serving God in a special way.

A famous meeting occurs when the two great founders of
religious orders, St. Francis and St. Dominic, meet at the house
of Cardinal Ugolino. The saints approached Ugolino together to ask
him not to look for candidates for bishoprics from among
their brethren.

ST. FRANCIS PREACHES REFORM

Of all God's saints there is no other who has been so universally beloved by people of all denominations, and there are few, who have more closely resembled Christ Himself, than the "little poor man of Assisi." Francis Bernardone was the son of a rich cloth merchant of Assisi in Italy. He was baptized John, but he came to be known as Francesco, "the Frenchman," because he spoke French so fluently, having learned it from his mother. As a youth, Francis was gay, extravagant, and popular. He loved music, poetry, and adventure. Every night he and his companions roamed the streets of Assisi, stopping to eat and drink at every tavern. Francis was kind and generous, however, and was frequently scolded by his father for taking rolls of cloth from the shop and selling them to get money for the poor.

After a lingering illness, Francis became more serious. One day, as he was praying before a crucifix in an abandoned chapel, he saw a vision of Christ so close and real that Francis held his breath with love and fear. "Go home, Francis," said Christ gently. "Go hence and build up my house. It is falling down." Francis understood that Christ wanted him to restore the Christian Church, which was falling into decay. He changed his rich clothing for a rough gray garment with a rope girdle and began to beg his way from door to door. He had always hated dirt and disorder and all the miseries of poverty. Now he accepted them all for

Christ. He forced himself to go to the leper colony, and he kissed the hands of the lepers as he gave them alms. He preached the Gospel and lived by its word, in utter poverty, barefooted and preaching repentance "with words which were like fire, penetrating the heart." Francis' extraordinary personality and his radically new approach to Christ drew followers by the hundreds.

In 1210 Innocent III gave verbal approval to the rule that Francis had drawn up, and it was solemnly ratified in 1223 by Pope Honorius III. Some of the Friars became priests and were known as the First Order. Francis would never consent to becoming a priest, thinking himself unworthy of such an honor. The Second Order for women, known as the Poor Clares, was founded by St. Clare of Assisi, the daughter of a rich and noble family. Like the Friars, they fasted much, wore coarse habits, slept on boards, and begged in order to serve the poor. Both the First and Second Orders grew in numbers almost miraculously and spread all over Europe. Later, a Third Order was established to admit lay people who wanted to sanctify their lives.

At one time Francis made a pilgrimage to Jerusalem and established a little community of Franciscans at the Holy Sepulcher. In his zeal he went to the camp of the Moslems, hoping to convert their leader. He did not accomplish the conversion, but the ruler treated Francis very kindly and made over to him the guardianship of the Holy Sepulcher. (The Holy Places are still in the custody of the Franciscans.) In 1224, on the feast of the Exaltation of the Cross, Francis received the Stigmata, marks of wounds like those of Our Lord. Two years later he died, lying on the ground amid poor and bare surroundings. He was canonized in 1228 by Pope Gregory IX. The very strict Franciscan rule was lightened in later years, and eventually three branches, of varying strictness, evolved: the Friars Minor, as the original friars were called, the Friars Minor Conventual, and the Friars Minor Capuchin, all of which still exist.

St. Francis and his companions receive
approval of the Rule from Pope Innocent III.

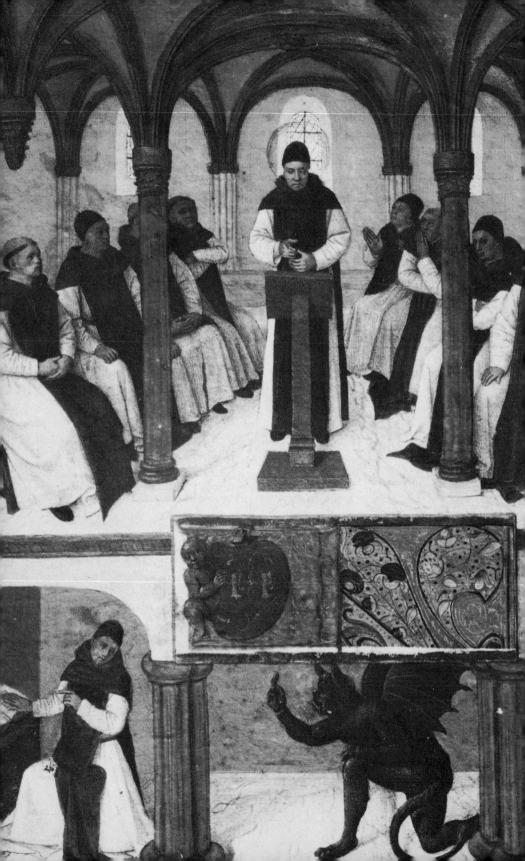

THE SCHOOLMEN

During the thirteenth century a new kind of scholar came into being, a man who brought the clear light of intellect to bear upon the problems of God, man, and the universe, in a way that had never been done before. Artists began to look at the world in a different way, and such men as Cimabue and Giotto tried experiments with space, color, light, and form. Up to this time practically all literature had been written in Latin or Greek. Now the vernacular, or common language of the people, began to take its place as a means of literary expression.

Perhaps the greatest intellectual achievement of the age was the extraordinary system known as scholasticism. The first scholastics had appeared in the eighth century with the great English scholar, the Venerable Bede, and his pupil Alcuin, whom Charlemagne called upon to help organize an educational system and prepare an authentic version of the Holy Scriptures. Now, in the thirteenth century, scholasticism, which is a fusion of philosophy and theology, became the basis of Christian thinking. The men who developed it were chiefly Dominicans, including Albert the Great and Thomas Aquinas, and Franciscans, among whom were St. Bonaventure, Roger Bacon, Raymond Lully, and Duns Scotus. Unafraid of looking for the truth wherever it might be found, they searched through the writings of the classical Greeks as well as those of their own contemporaries among Mohammedans and Jews. These sources contributed to the great body of medieval Christian thought of which Thomas Aquinas was the chief architect. One of his books, the *Summa Theologica,* still forms the core of Catholic philosophical studies.

St. Thomas lectured both at the University of Paris and at the papal school for outstanding scholars which accompanied the pope in his travels. In the bottom panel of this picture the devil is trying—hopelessly—to subvert the saint's clearminded attack on philosophical problems. Thomas died on the way to attend the Council of Lyons.

St. Thomas took such a deep approach to philosophy and theology that he was often misunderstood by his contemporaries, who could not grasp the subtleties of his mind, and there was some opposition to his thinking. However, during his lifetime, a gathering of doctors of the Church, in the Council of Anagni in 1256 (ABOVE) under Pope Alexander IV, vindicated his teachings. After his

death further opposition arose and several propositions drawn from his works were condemned by different authorities; for a time the Franciscan Order forbade its members to study his works. However, four years after Thomas's death, the General Chapter of the Dominicans officially imposed his teachings on the Order, and in 1323 he was canonized by John XXII.

The pilgrimage was one of the most popular of all medieval devotions. Many pilgrims made the long trip to the Holy Land, where they were likely also to visit St. Catherine's monastery on Mount Sinai. Others journeyed to Rome or to Santiago de Compostela in Spain. But even local pilgrimages were popular, such as the one to Canterbury (ABOVE). LEFT: exhausted pilgrimages sprawl on the ground before the shrine of our Lady of Ratisbonne.

Along with the universities, the monasteries
were great centers of learning. At the
Benedictine monastery of Tavara in Spain
monks are shown in the scriptorium
working with compasses on mathematical
problems. In the tower other monks are
about to ring the bells for the Divine Office.
BELOW: *monks at Citeaux still
follow the ancient Benedictine tradition
almost unchanged.*

THE PREVALENCE OF WITCHES

One curious and disturbing aspect of the Middle Ages was the prevalence of persons who were called witches and who actually did practice witchcraft. Nearly all rural areas had their old crones who were supposed to deal with the devil and who were believed to lay spells on people. Many of those accused of witchcraft were the still-pagan descendants of old families which had never been converted. They passed on the ancient rites from one generation to another, chiefly among the poor, although there were also cases of witchcraft among the well-to-do.

Certain common features marked European witchcraft. One widespread practice was the worship of a horned deity like those worshiped in ancient India, Greece, Egypt, Rome, and other places. In the seventh century in England, authorities denounced anyone who went about wearing a mask that resembled a stag, a bull, or any other wild animal. Three centuries later King Edgar discovered that the Old Religion, as paganism was called, was more common than the Christian faith and urged fervent religious instruction of the young. The old cult held on tenaciously, however, throughout the Middle Ages. Dozens of witches were tried

Three witches are burned at the stake (to the dismay of the devil flying overhead), while in the background a fourth is beheaded.

and burned; yet they continued to flourish and worship pagan idols.

The witches were usually organized in groups of thirteen under the charge of a horned leader to whom homage was paid at their meetings on the Witches' Sabbath. Ritual meals were eaten and certain drugs like belladonna or a particular kind of mushroom were used to induce strange fancies and actions. Sometimes the witches actually believed that they could fly, and their antics led to the familiar notion of witches riding on brooms. Most witches lived by themselves with animal companions and used herbs and charms when they were called by Christian peasants to act as healers or fortunetellers. Burning at the stake was the common fate of condemned witches.

Official attitudes toward witches changed over the centuries. Charlemagne forbade the persecution of witches, and so did many early bishops. Pope Gregory VII ruled against the killing of old women for supposed crimes, such as causing storms, but by the fourteenth century witches were being hunted down by the Inquisition and many mistakes were made. (The case of Joan of Arc is a notable example.) The Protestant reformers, especially in England, were also deeply concerned with the stamping out of witchcraft, and some of the greatest persecutions must be attributed to them.

A popular scene in the medieval imagination was that of witches flying. Here, three in animal guise are about to take off for the Witches' Sabbath.

The right of sanctuary was a privilege often used in the Middle Ages. By seeking refuge in a church, where he had to touch a certain object, either the altar (in early times) or, as in the abbey at Hexham, England, the frith or sanctuary stool, a criminal would be free from arrest or pursuit by enemies. At Durham the petitioner, once he had placed both hands on the knocker (LEFT), was admitted to the cathedral by the monks for thirty-seven days, at the end of which time he could either take his chances in escaping or devote the remainder of his life to the service of the Church. In most cases, however, a criminal was given forty days in which to take an oath of abjuration and be escorted to a seaport to go into exile; otherwise he might be forcibly extricated. (The privilege was not extended to sacrilege or high treason.) At the Reformation the right of sanctuary was curtailed and was finally abolished.

PERSECUTION OF THE JEWS

The Jews occupied a special position in medieval life. Both protected and abused at various times, they alternated between freedom and despair. They had been fairly free from persecution during the growth of the new nations in the Dark Ages, but by the time of the crusades their position had changed, and during the First Crusade one army of knights was guilty of slaughtering Jews all along their route to Byzantium.

The Jews were denied ownership of land and barred from most occupations except petty trading and money-lending. Christians were not supposed to engage in money-lending, although the new merchant princes were beginning to do so. The Jews segregated themselves into separate streets and areas, which later came to be known as ghettos, at first voluntarily, but later by order. The custom became a civil law, and the ghettos were surrounded by walls. The inhabitants had to be inside by a certain hour at night or suffer penalties. Popular rumor often charged Jews with imaginary crimes. Sometimes they were forced to "confess" under torture and even put to death. In 1247, after 34 Jews had been put to death under false charges and later proved innocent, the Jews of France and Germany begged Pope Innocent IV to defend them against such accusations. He confirmed that the charges were false and forbade any such trials in the future. Other popes did the same, but similar incidents persisted for centuries.

King John of England was one of the worst offenders. He restricted Jews to 25 towns so that they could easily be registered and taxed and forbade them to leave England because they were a valuable source of income. A few years after these laws went

German Jews of the thirteenth century, like those of most European countries, wore a distinctive dress.

into effect, their privilege of lending money was restricted, thus depriving them of their principal means of support. Destitute, the Jews were finally driven out entirely in 1290, and their presence in England was illegal for 400 years. Later they were expelled from France, Spain, and Portugal. In 1264, the generous Boleslaus the Pious opened Poland to Jewish refugees.

*A popular medieval sport was pitting a learned rabbi
against Christian theologians. If the rabbi won the dispute,
he was likely to lose his life; if he deliberately argued
poorly, or was insufficiently skilled, he lost the
respect of his own community. Here, Susskind of Trimberg
appears before a bishop and his aides.*

The Inquisition began in 1233 under Gregory IX when the Pope appointed a tribunal of members of the mendicant orders —chiefly Dominicans and Franciscans—to rout out heresy and bring about a return to the true Faith. In the past the discovery and punishment of heretics had usually been initiated by the princes or by an aroused public. Originally a means to insure a fair trial for the accused and to keep him from abuse by secular powers, the Inquisition drifted into progressively harsher methods. At first an obstinate heretic was punished by imprisonment; but soon the use of torture was also introduced, and unrepentant heretics were turned over to the secular arm for execution. The scene at the right shows the various stages of a trial before the Inquisition (presided over by St. Dominic), ending with a Dominican attempting to console three despondent heretics awaiting their turn at the stake.

NEW WORLDS ARE DISCOVERED

In 1271 a group of Venetian merchants named Polo set out on a trading expedition into the Far East, taking with them two Dominican friars to go as missionaries to the court of the famous founder of the Mongol dynasty in China, Kublai Khan. The older Polos, who had already traveled in this area, were friends of the Khan. He had expressed an interest in Christianity and had asked the pope to send him a hundred learned men to teach both Christianity and the seven arts. Young Marco Polo became a favorite of the Khan and served him on business matters in China and India. After seventeen years in the East, the Polos started home and returned to Venice in time for Marco to join the Venetian forces fighting Genoa. He was taken prisoner and while in captivity dictated an account of his travels to a fellow prisoner. Polo was still in a state of amazement at the splendors he had observed and experienced, and his book was largely factual. It has ever since been of great value to historians and for several centuries was the most reliable guide to many parts of the Far East.

The Polos set off from Venice on their
daring expedition into the Far East.

Pope Boniface VIII as he looked during the Holy Year.

THE FIRST HOLY YEAR

As the year 1299 drew to a close, a vast crowd assembled in St. Peter's Basilica for Christmas Eve Vespers. Many of the worshipers were pilgrims from other countries attracted by a rumor that various indulgences could be obtained during the coming year by all who visited the tombs of St. Peter and St. Paul. After Christmas the number of pilgrims increased. The tombs of the saints were besieged, and the streets of Rome were so crowded that it was almost impossible to walk through them.

Finally the pope, Boniface VIII, questioned a man who was 107 years old and was being carried in the arms of his sons to see the veil of St. Veronica. "I remember," said the pilgrim, "that at the beginning of the last century, my father, who was a laborer, came to Rome and stayed here as long as his means lasted in order to gain the indulgence. He told me not to forget to come at the beginning of the next century if I should live so long." Two other pilgrims over a hundred years old and a number of other elderly persons confirmed his statement. Although no written document in support of the belief could be discovered, it was apparent that from oral testimony the people were expecting special blessings in the opening years of the new century. Unwilling that his people should be deprived of what they had tried so hard and at such inconvenience to obtain, Boniface proclaimed a Holy Year, the first officially on record.

an age of chaos

Few centuries have seen such change as did the fourteenth. About the middle of the century, a devastating plague, the Black Death, swept across Europe, bringing in its wake a vast disruption of society. Church, state, city, and countryside were affected. People died by tens of thousands. The plague's one beneficial

The Conquest of Death—carrying away good and evil alike—is illustrated in a manuscript which draws its inspiration from the continual recurrence of the plague in late Middle Ages.

result was a gradual bettering of the life of the peasants, often by way of rebellion and by a rejection of traditional doctrines. At the same time, the Church was rent by a deep cleavage that divided Europe into opposing camps, with rival popes in Rome and Avignon, and shook the wavering faith of millions. The ravages of plague and the disturbances caused by religious division paved the way for the Reformation, the rumblings of which had been heard for generations.

*The plague kept coming back. In this
fifteenth-century painting a priest
reads the burial service over
plague victims, while in heaven
St. Sebastian intercedes for them.*

THE BLACK DEATH

In 1349, a German writer named Jacob von Königshofen sadly
took up his pen and began a record of the frightful events that
had taken place that year. "There occurred," wrote Jacob, "the
greatest epidemic that ever happened. Death went from one end
of the earth to the other, on that side and this side of the sea, and
it was greater among the Saracens than among the Christians. In
some lands everyone died so that no one was left. Ships were
also found on the seas laden with wares; the crew had all died
and no one guided the ship. The bishop of Marseilles and priests
and monks died, and more than half the people there died with
them. In other kingdoms and cities so many people perished that
it would be horrible to describe. The pope at Avignon stopped all
sessions of court, locked himself in a room, allowed no one to
approach him, and had a fire burning before him all the time.
And from what this epidemic came, all wise teachers and physi-
cians could only say that it was God's will. And as the plague was
now here, so was it in other places, and lasted more than a whole
year. This epidemic also came to Strasbourg in the summer of the
above-mentioned year, and it is estimated that about 16,000
people died."

The plague had started in Constantinople. Each case was marked by a high fever, and invariably the result was death. This was the West's introduction to the disastrous epidemic known as the Bubonic Plague or the Black Death. It soon swept over Europe, destroying almost all before it. It has been estimated that the death toll was as high as three-quarters of the population. This extremely contagious disease was carried by rat fleas that had become infected from biting diseased rats.

The plague spread rapidly across the Mediterranean, reaching England by 1349. Following the trade routes, it crossed Germany and Scandinavia and invaded Poland from the west. Every level of society was affected, and there was no escape. The nobles died as quickly as the peasants. Towns were emptied. Without teachers or pupils, the school system fell into decay. Communication and trade came to a halt. The number of religious declined. Since the peasantry was reduced by half, there was great competition for labor, and in England a law was passed freezing wages of laborers at the pre-plague level. The result was an increase of tension between rich and poor. About one-third of the population of Europe was carried off during the first three years of the plague. What was worse, it continued to return almost every ten years, thus halting the continuous increase in population. In Germany the panic was accompanied by an outburst of persecution against the Jews, who were accused of causing the plague. Many of their communities were destroyed and the survivors fled to the East. Systematic attempts were made to check the epidemic. Quarantines were established, victims segregated in hospitals, and special doctors and health commissioners were appointed, but little improvement resulted. Frequent wars and long sieges had seriously interfered with sanitation and had increased the communication of disease. All across Europe came a lowering of standards. It was a long time before the effects of the Black Death were erased from the physical and moral life of the people.

SCHISM DIVIDES THE CHURCH

The great schism of Avignon divided the Church for a period of thirty-five years and helped to plant the seeds of the Reformation. There was no question of faith or practice involved. The schism was entirely a matter of people and politics, of human vanity, and self-interest. Avignon, a commercial city in southern France, was so attractive that Pope Urban V (1367–70) chose to move the papal court there from Rome. When his successor, Gregory IX (the last French pope) was elected, he was strongly urged by a great many people, including two famous saints, Brigid of Sweden and Catherine of Siena, to re-establish the papal headquarters at Rome. There were, of course, strong supporters for Avignon, and the Italians appeared none too anxious to have the papacy return, but Gregory finally moved back. The events after his death led to the Great Schism.

The Romans feared that the papal court would now return to Avignon. The mob demanded a Roman, or at least an Italian, pope. On April 8, 1378, the sixteen cardinals present elected Urban VI. The new pope began very badly, offending even his friends, and it was later determined that he was probably mentally incompetent. The cardinals slipped out of Rome and declared unanimously that Urban's election had not been valid, having been carried out in fear of the mob. They elected Robert of Geneva as Pope Clement VII. The next year Clement fled from Italy back to Avignon. Consequently there were two popes, Urban in Rome and Clement in Avignon, each claiming to be the true pope, and each supported by different national factions, and eventually two lines of succession.

This state of affairs naturally caused infinite trouble and confusion. In 1409 Europe's leading ecclesiastics met at Pisa in Italy to try to solve the problem. They only complicated matters still further, however. Pope Gregory XII was now the pope in Rome and Benedict XIII in Avignon. The council, which actually had no real authority to act, declared both popes heretical and elected Alexander V, with the result that there were three claimants to the throne of Peter. Alexander's successor, the anti-pope John XXIII (an anti-pope is one elected illegally in opposition to one elected properly, or canonically, by the college of cardinals), gained the allegiance of a great many people all over Europe. In 1414 he convened the Council of Constance, of which some of its 45 sessions are recognized as the sixteenth ecumenical council. The reforms it voted were minor, considering the problems facing the Christian world, but it did settle the question of Avignon.

Gregory XII, the Roman pope, resigned, and John and Benedict, both of whom refused to step down, were deposed. Martin V was then elected by the council. This election was supported by all of Europe, and the Great Schism was at an end. The major result of the long division was to delay the great reforms that were so badly needed by the Church. Most Catholic historians now agree that the Roman line was the true canonical line, and the title John XXIII was again taken by Angelo Roncalli in 1958.

Elected pope at the Council of Constance in 1417, Martin V rides to his coronation with the Holy Roman Emperor Sigismund holding his bridle.

A NEW LITERATURE THROUGH DANTE

In spite of plagues and religious controversy, arts and letters continued to develop and flourish in the fourteenth century. Perhaps the most typical of his time was Dante Alighieri, one of the greatest names in all literature. (He was born in Florence, Italy, in 1265.) Dante liked political life, and he vigorously opposed all abuses of power or riches, particularly corruption in the Church. In his *Divine Comedy,* he placed many famous people in hell for their sins. In another poem he set forth the idea that the civil authority of the emperor is derived from God and is therefore exercised independently of the pope.

Up to Dante's time, most medieval literature had been written in Provençal, the language used in the lyrics of the troubadours. Dante, however, used the Florentine dialect of his native city and thus gave Italy a national language, in which his works are still read today.

Dante stands before the walls of Florence, holding LA COMMEDIA
*in his hand. At the left, devils drive the souls of the damned
into Hell. In the rear, other souls work out their salvation on
the hill of Purgatory. An angel marks the heads of newcomers
with the sins to be expiated, while others reach the summit
of the hill and the earthly paradise
symbolized by Adam and Eve.*

The only known true-life portrait of Joan. Her case was later reopened; in 1456 she was completely rehabilitated.

JOAN OF ARC IS BURNED

In 1426 a young peasant girl named Joan, who lived in the village of Domrémy, began to hear angelic voices as she tended her flocks in the fields and thought about the unhappy state of her country. The dukes of Burgundy and Orleans were fighting for the crown. She prayed that God would bless the true king, Charles, and permit him to be crowned in the old royal city of Rheims. Joan had always dearly loved St. Margaret and St. Catherine, and she had a great devotion to St. Michael, too. Now she began to hear their voices telling her that it was God's will that she go to the king and help him.

Charles VII, commonly known as the Dauphin, was a rather frivolous and not very forceful young man. When Joan, in answer to her voices, put on a soldier's uniform and went to one of the French generals, she was sent home at first, but Charles believed in her. A number of theologians examined Joan but could find nothing wrong with her. They advised Charles to make prudent use of her services. At last, clad in white armor, Joan rode at the head of the French troops to the city of Orleans, which was al-

ihs

C ma
ap
gla
et
fes

cou

que

roy

a)

w

MECREDI C

ready surrounded by the English. In the battle that followed, the English were defeated. There were further victories under Joan's leadership, and in the same year, 1429, she saw her king crowned in Rheims.

The crowning was all that Joan had been promised by her voices, and now things began to go badly for her. She was captured by the Duke of Burgundy on May 23, 1430. He kept her prisoner until late in the fall and then sold her to the English. Charles made no attempt to save her by ransom or by force. The English, who were still smarting at their defeat by an army led by a girl, made false charges against her. They accused her of being disloyal to the Church and to the pope. They wanted to put her to death, but they pretended to give her a just trial first, on charges of heresy and witchcraft. Their real purpose was to discredit Charles and his clergy. They were able to bribe certain French priests to act as a court. Alone and without counsel, Joan defended herself with amazing skill, and she refused to retract her story about the holy voices. The judges condemned her as a heretic, and on May 29, 1431, the faithful Joan, barely nineteen years old, was burned at the stake.

Upon Joan's request, a Dominican friar holds a cross before her eyes. Her last words were: "Jesus! Jesus!" Her ashes were scattered into the Seine. An English witness cried, "We are lost; we have burned a saint!"

THE PEASANTS BEGIN TO REVOLT

Near the end of the fourteenth century, 100,000 English peasants revolted under the leadership of an obscure worker called Wat the Tyler because he worked on roofs. For thirty years their wages had been frozen by the Statute of Laborers first instituted after the Black Death. Now new and unjust taxes were being imposed. Certain speakers, among them John Wyclif, a fanatical religious reformer, and John Ball, an excommunicated priest, excited the people to fury. They began by murdering the archbishop of Canterbury. Then, with the mob increasing at every corner, Tyler led the rebels on to London. The king, Richard II, avoided meeting them at first, but they sacked the city and finally forced him to listen. They made him promise to abolish serfdom and all kinds of feudal service, as well as market monopolies and restrictions on buying and selling. He also promised pardon to all the rebels. Tyler was not yet satisfied. He had several high officials executed in the Tower of London. The disorders continued throughout the city as Tyler met again with the king to present new demands. During the talks a bystander made some remark that infuriated Tyler, who drew his dagger. In the scuffle that followed, Wat Tyler was mortally wounded by the mayor of London and died on the spot. King Richard, with a great show of courage, kept the mob at bay until the mayor was able to bring up reinforcements. Then, leaderless and bewildered, the rebels broke, and the revolt which had raged all over England was speedily put down with extreme cruelty. The king revoked all his promises, and the unhappy peasants returned to their homes defeated.

John Ball, the heretic priest (on horseback), and Wat Tyler, leader of the revolt, join armies in the peasants' rebellion of 1381.

WYCLIF AGAINST THE CHURCH

John Wyclif, who had roused the English peasants into revolting, was by birth a Yorkshireman. It was he, as much as any man, who brought about the Reformation. His Bible, translated from the Vulgate, was the first full version in English, and a major accomplishment. He was a clear and vigorous speaker, and he preached heresies that had been undermining the orthodox doctrines of Christianity for centuries. Wyclif insisted that all authority lay in the Scriptures alone, and declared the right of all to have access to them. He attacked the doctrine of transubstantiation and denied that the sacraments of the Church are necessary to obtain God's grace. At first Wyclif had enjoyed the favor and protection of the English court and the parliament, but when the common people actually tried to carry out his teachings and revolt against the wealthy landowners as in the case of Wat Tyler's mob, they turned against him. He was condemned as a heretic in 1380 and again in 1382 and was deprived of his professorship at Oxford by royal order. Nevertheless his teachings spread to the continent of Europe and exerted great influence on John Hus of Bohemia, a professor at the University of Prague, and through him upon a young man named Martin Luther, who began as an Augustinian monk and ended up by starting the German Reformation.

Twenty years after his death, Wyclif's bones are exhumed, burned and thrown into the river. Public sympathy was with Wyclif during his life and he died peacefully in his own parish. It was only later that the crown turned against his doctrines.

The Bohemian priest John Hus was heavily influenced by Wyclif and translated many of his works into Czech. Hus's own teachings were soon denounced in Rome. Czech national feelings entered the scene, also complicated by opposing allegiances to the Roman and Avignon popes. Eventually Hus was excommunicated by the anti-pope John XXIII. Given a safe conduct to the Council of Constance, Hus was arrested and eventually tried. He died bravely at the stake on July 6, 1415 [LEFT], becoming a national hero. But the schism he introduced among his people persisted, and his doctrines were among the most powerful to affect the course of the Reformation.

THE PRINTING REVOLUTION

It was a German printer named Johann Gutenberg who by his remarkable discovery of movable type helped to revolutionize society and to bring about the end of the Middle Ages. For nearly 1500 years, the Christian monks had copied ancient manuscripts and copies of the Scriptures, sitting for endless hours in their cells and working slowly and painstakingly, first on parchment and later on paper. With the invention of printing, man received one of his greatest gifts. No longer was education and learning controlled entirely by the clergy and available only to the wealthy. Now, theoretically at least, every man could learn to read.

Gutenberg was born in Mainz in 1396 and was trained as a goldsmith. By 1448 he was experimenting with movable type cast in separate letters on which ink could be spread, making it possible to produce thousands of copies of a manuscript for every one that could be made by hand. Gutenberg became involved in financial difficulties and lost most of his property, but he did manage to produce a complete Bible in 1456. (It was known as the Mazarin Bible because Cardinal Mazarin was one of its owners.) This Bible, which was probably the first book printed in Europe, was an extremely beautiful work. It was issued in two volumes, each page printed in two columns with 42 lines to a column. Forty copies are known to have survived, of which only two are complete. In his old age Gutenberg was pensioned by the archbishop of Mainz and continued to work until he was 97.

The art of printing spread rapidly. Many printers learned their craft at Mainz where Gutenberg had established his shop. Next to the Bible, psalters, or books of psalms, and books about the Blessed Virgin were the most popular. The illustrations for all of these books were carved in wood and were used over and over again.

116

The first illustrated book to be printed in Italy (at Rome, in 1467) was the MEDITATIONES *of Johannes de Turrecremata. This page shows the Assumption.*

Irmiſſime credimus domine iheſu q̃ tu qui de bonorandis
parentibus legem hominibus tradidiſti·glorioſã matrẽ tuã
ius aſſũptione ita oimoda i corpore ⁊ aĩa illuſtraueris gloria·
bonore ſublimaueris·ut nulla mortalis lingua ualeat exprimeř
Quis eni cogitare ſufficiat q̃ bonorabiliter bodie regina mũdi p
eſſerit·quãto deuotionis affectu·tota in eius occurſu celeſtiũ legi
nũ ṗdierit multitudo·quãtis ad thronũ glorie canticis ſit deduc
a·q̃ placido uultu·q̃ ſerena facie q̃ diuinis amplexibus a filio ſit
aſcepta ⁊ ſup omnẽ creaturã exaltata Glorificemus ergo uirginẽ
quã bodie padiſus excepit gaudẽs·quã angeli cũ laudibus ṗſecũ
quã apłox chorus ueneraƚ·quã martires cãdidati beatificãt·quã
anctorũ cõfeſſorũ incolatus cõcelebrat numerus·cui bodie ſanc
orũ uirginũ cũ ſuis palmis iuictricibus exultans occurrit exerci
us·quoniã bec ẽ ṗ quã ois maledictio ſoluta eſt·⁊ celeſtis bene
ictio in totũ uenit mundũ·Clama ergo fidelis aĩa O maria ſtell
naris·dignitate ſingularis·in ſupremo ſita poli·nos cõmẽda tu
pli·ut tecum letemur in gloria·

POPULAR DEVOTIONS

In the fifteenth century very few people other than the clergy had any adequate sort of education. Simple devotional prints were widely used to help the ordinary layman understand his religion. They were used also by some of the poorer members of the clergy, who were themselves often inadequately educated. One such print, which portrays a giant hand, was used in 1466 as a guide to the examination of conscience. Mary Magdalen, identified by her jar of ointment, kneels above the thumb as the symbol of the repentant sinner. Facing her is another saint standing on a dragon, which represents evil, and carrying the vessels for sprinkling holy water on the dragon to subdue him. For those able to read Latin, there are two short stanzas beside the wrist which explain the symbolism of the five fingers and tell what must be done to make a good confession.

Si voluntatem dei scis,
Agnosce malum ut euites.
Si malum egisti, doleas.
Si vere doles, confitearis.
Si confessus es, satisfac.

Polex significat voluntatem dei.
Index significat cognitionem.
Medius digitus significat contricionem.
Medicus significat confessionem.
Auricularis satisfactionem.

When thou knowest the will of the Lord,
Then own the faults in order to avoid them.
When thou hast done evil, then repent of it.
When thou verily repentest, then confess it.
When thou hast confessed, then do penance.

The thumb signifies God's will.
The forefinger signifies the examination.
The middle-finger signifies the repentance.
The ring-finger signifies the confession.
The ear-finger signifies the satisfaction.

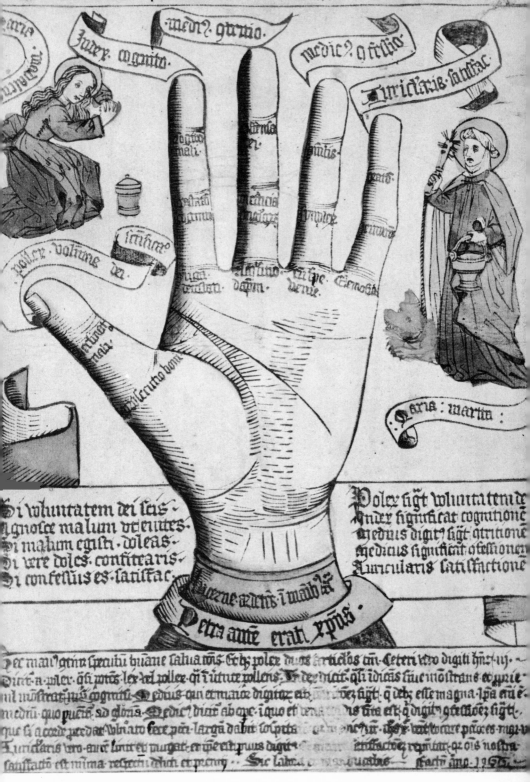

THE WICKEDNESS OF VENICE

The centuries between the medieval period of history and that which we call modern are usually known as the Renaissance, which means a rebirth. It did, indeed, seem that the world was building itself anew. Life was rich and exciting and beautiful. The arts flourished. The Church itself, in its exterior aspects, grew ever more magnificent. Toward the end of the fifteenth century, great processions for the feast of Corpus Christi, for example, were popular manifestations of man's devotion to God. In times of crisis the people paraded daily, imploring heaven to intercede; often they went barefoot and fasting and weeping.

Nevertheless, in Venice, a city where men could so proudly pro-

*A procession around Venice's Great Piazza on the Feast of
Corpus Christi was painted by Gentile Bellini in 1496.*

claim their love of God, the city fathers kept an official poisoner
to get rid of enemies. Attempts were made at poisoning the Holy
Roman Emperor, popes, kings, sultans, bishops, and a host of
minor personages. The Venetians even waged germ warfare against
enemies, using agents who carried bubonic plague. Not only
Venice, but nearly every city, abounded in plots and assassinations
and carried on wars of violence and pillage. In 1478, an attempt
was made to poison two young princes, Lorenzo and Guiliano
Medici, then the heads of the famous Medici family, wealthy
bankers and patrons of the arts. An archbishop and two priests
were involved in the plot. When it failed, a decision was made to
stab the brothers to death at High Mass in the cathedral of
Florence. The hired professional murderers succeeded in splitting
Guiliano's skull as he knelt before the high altar. Lorenzo escaped.

121

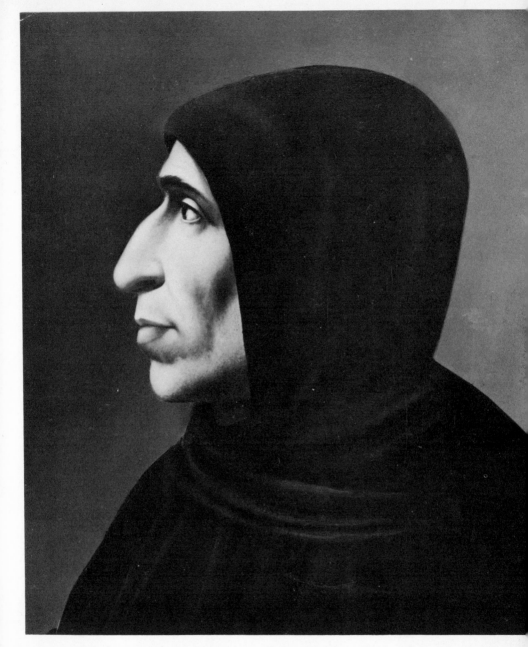

The worldliness of Christians did not go unchallenged. Toward the end of the fifteenth century the Dominican friar Girolomo Savanarola [ABOVE] achieved great fame in Florence by denouncing the immorality of both clergy and laity and preaching repentance. He prophesied on the future, sometimes with startling accuracy. His success brought him to the attention of the notorious Pope Alexander VI [LEFT], who demanded that Savanarola come to Rome for investigation; the monk refused; Alexander forbade him to preach further, a command ignored by Savanarola, who was then excommunicated. His position deteriorated rapidly after that, and, in 1498, he was hanged in the Florence market place, venerated by some as a saint, despised by others as a fanatic.

The mighty secular spirit of the Renaissance, the vital, splendid concern with art and letters, reached right into the papal court— indeed the popes themselves were the leading patrons of scholars, artists and poets. The rediscovery of classical forms, including the works of Homer, Plato and Aristotle, and Horace, Cicero and Ovid, the finding of buried Roman statuary, the arrival of learned refugees from Byzantium—all contributed to the reaction against the barbarousness of earlier times (for which the phrase "The Dark Ages" was coined). Raphael's painting of a pope surrounded by cherubs and a classical nymph is indicative of the almost pagan frame of mind into which even the Church was sinking.

"GOD HIMSELF WILL INTERVENE"

Thoughtful men, observing the behavior of the people and the corruption of the Church, predicted that the time for punishment was not far away. Pope Leo X was one of the chief offenders. He appointed his cardinals for personal and political reasons, receiving rich rewards, and he permitted all kinds of crime to flourish. "If Leo leaves crimes unpunished any longer," wrote Pico della Mirandola, a scholar of that period, "God himself will intervene." And the great English bishop, St. John Fisher, commented: "If the pope will not reform the Curia, God will find means to do it." A collective Judas was at work within the Church, and no one seemed able to halt the impending disasters.

INDEX

PICTURE SOURCES

ALINARI: *19, 71, 105, 121, 124*

P. M. BARDI: *16–17*

BIPS: *32*

BRITISH INFORMATION SERVICE: *84*

BRITISH MUSEUM: *77, 111*

BURGER BIBLIOTHEK, BERN: *38*

J. A. FORTIER: *28, 30, 79*

FRENCH GOVERNMENT TOURIST OFFICE: *2–3, 7, 13, 15*

GUTHLAC ROLL: *9, 65*

LATERAN MUSEUM: *41*

JEAN MARIE MARCEL: *27*

METROPOLITAN MUSEUM: *58–59, 61, 117*

NATIONAL GALLERY OF ART: *18*

PIERPONT MORGAN LIBRARY: *78*

PRADO MUSEUM: *91*

EDWARD RICE: *31, 52*

D. VAN NOSTRAND CO.: *74–75*

WALTERS ART GALLERY: *99*